The Rhythm
My Everyday Life

by
Kishma Adams

Copyright © 2014 Kishma Adams
Printed in USA by Greater Is He Publishing

Editor: Shari Armstrong
Cover Design: Robert King
Interior Layout: Tony Bradford

All rights reserved. No part of this book may be reproduced or transmitted in any form or by any means without written permission from the author.

ISBN: 978-1-938950-48-3

Greater Is He Publishing
9824 E. Washington St.
Chagrin Falls, Ohio 44023
Phone: 216.288.9315

www.GreaterIsHePublishing.com

CONTENTS

Pretty Handsome Man..	1
Letting Go..	4
Love...	6
Grocery Store Clerk...	8
Lightning and Thunder...	10
Storm..	11
Feelings..	12
Rhythm...	14
My Imagination Running Wild..............................	16
Legend..	18
Determination...	19
Ghetto Love..	20
Spontaneous..	22
Beauty is in the Eyes of the Beholder...................	23
Dominate the Challenge..	24
Virginity...	25
Yes, Let Us Know..	27
Disappointment..	29
The Love of Languages..	31
Friendship...	32
Poem...	33
Missing Affection...	34
Dirty Church Member..	35

30 Days	37
The Clear Blue Sky	39
Emotions	40
Life Shell	41
Rhyme	43
Infatuation	45
Slow of Speech	46
Thug Passion	47
Remember the Night Forever	49
Lust	51
Backbone	53
Trauma	55
Urban	58
Cry	60
Sincere	61
Eternal Love Forever	63
The Thirteen-Year-Old	65
Emotions	66
Sticks and Stones	67
Rap is Poetry	68
War	69
Double Lesson	70
True Life Poetry	71
Sense of Humor	72
Until Death Do Us Part	73
My First Option	75

Valedictorian...	77
One Flesh..	78
Hoping, Dreaming, and Wishing.......................	80
Aqua Fallso...	82
Mercy...	83
From the Inside and Out.................................	84
Don't...	86

Pretty Handsome Man

I used to leave my house at 11:36 am, because I knew I would eventually run into him. He is a pretty handsome man, his skin complexion is the color of sand. It's amazing how God created him to live on his green land. He has a mysterious look in his hazel eyes. If you have a serious conversation with him, the words that come out of his mouth can sometimes be nice. His handsome looks will never tell any lies. One day I hope I meet a man like him, then when I do he will definitely be mine. I think about this hard working man all the time. Listen to my rhyme, because I do believe that love is blind. Poetry can be full of meaning, things in life happen for a reason. Looks are very deceiving, but looking at this man can be very pleasing. My love could never be full of lies. The moment of being in his presence gave me so many butterflies, my lustful heart felt like it was about to jump out of my body. Thank God I never had the opportunity to get close to him, because if that happened, I would have become very naughty. The pretty color hazel did not come from any of the colors of the rainbow. Let me put the truth on the table. This pretty handsome man has curls and waves. One time he got his hair cut in a nice fad. But, I think about him almost every day. Some way, some how he told me his first name. The thoughts of him just flow through my brain.

I never had a chance to be in a relationship with the guys that I loved, so that formed a whole bunch of pain. He is so sweet, like the lovely rain. His voice sounds like a pleasant echo, and he also has freckles. He always has on a work uniform so his pants are always buckled. His hair is light brown, like a king wearing a crown. He drives his bus around town and he never slows down. I would love to have a man like him in my life right now. It seems like a girl from every different race is always up in his face, they probably be expecting him to ask them out on a date. Every time I stood at the bus stop at 11:36 am, just thinking about him increased different speeds in my heart rate. No matter where I was going, I was never late. Even when I felt disappointed about something, I never show any animosity or hate. This man is below the average height, but that never stops me from thinking about him every night. When it was time for me to get off the bus, I always looked him in the eye and told him goodbye. But one thing I will tell you, I never thought one day I would fall in love with an older guy.

Letting Go

It's very difficult to watch the love of your life get buried into the ground, especially if you're eight months pregnant and your belly is round. This man proposed to you. I bet you had plans of walking down the aisle with a splendid white gown. As soon as you found out he got shot in the head, you screamed out loud. Now a big piece of your heart is dim. As a mother, you will have to teach his son how to shoot a basketball above the rim. Losing your soul mate must have felt like being a rose without a stem. The time that you were pregnant with his child, his reactions in his face looked so proud. He looked forward to seeing his firstborn wrapped in a small towel. Letting a person go is like watching them drive down the road, where a good spirit will automatically take their soul. At the end, you're stuck in a double lesson. You will have to be both parents to his son, that's beautiful and precious.

Love

Love is a feeling with deep affection, it can make your heart feel like a lock with secure protection, passionate desire is a historical legend. Rapture can be beautiful like a fashion magazine. A man can get on his knees and offer the woman of his dreams a beautiful diamond ring. Endearment was created from the Lord, our King. The moment of making unconditional love to your partner, they may feel like a beautiful white dove. Sex is emotional. It's supposed to bring two people together so they can love each other even more. Love is like an eagle that cruises through the air and soars. A broken heart will make you walk out of the door. Old sailors fell deeply in love with mermaids, that comb their hair on the ocean shore. Thunder and lightning can form into a storm. Making love in a tub, the water can be very warm. In my lonely eyes, love is a dream. Imagine hurting the only person you love, then the next morning that person is never seen. What if they died and flew away, like an angel with their magical wings.

Grocery Store Clerk

Having a split personality is like changing a song into a totally different melody. I have known this grocery store clerk for a long time. The day he laid eyes on me, he told me that I looked nice. The moment of hearing those words was a very big surprise. Every time I walk inside of the grocery store, I can sense his presence, looking right at me when I walk through the door. I'm so curious about him, I wonder if a guy like him would ever be the one. I would have to be absolutely sure. I had a short conversion with him, and he sounded so mature. I remember telling him I went to church to pray, to make a testimony, so God can cast my sins away. He asked me what was the topic today. Then I said to forgive and forget. If you have faith in Jesus, He will heal the weak and the sick. I'm gonna have to admit, this grocery store clerk introduced himself to me and he told me his name, and it's definitely not Rick. He is a good looking young man. I hope he has a successful plan. We did not meet each other last year. Sometimes this grocery store clerk works the cashier. When I stand in the grocery store line, the things that he says to me always make me feel fine. Deep down inside, I know this grocery store clerk wants to tell me what's on his mind, because every time I stand in his face, his whole personality begins to shine. The days that my dad and I go grocery shopping there's no way I could avoid his attention. This boy will keep trying. If he and I ever got together, then things didn't work out between this grocery store clerk and me. What is the point of crying? Because through the power of God, I feel like a bird that keeps on soaring and flying.

Lightning and Thunder

Lightning is like fighting to have a good hiding spot, when stranded in the darkness of thunder, day and night. Thunder is like hearing the sound of the ocean shore king roar. In the north, thunder is like having wonder under the after life people will get caught playing dice when Christ comes back. Living in a world of thunder every day can be so curl. It reminds me of pulling a disease out of the body of the innocent, that will some day be healed by the hands of God. My entire life is full of wonder. I'm in a hurry to overcome my worries. The other half of my life is full of lightning, evil tries to attack my appearances. My intellect is very serious about when I want my curiosity to get physical, but I'm not going to take it far and that's a miracle.

Storm

The sound of thunder places my mind into so much wonder. The sun begins hiding behind the roar of lightning. A storm can be fatal, the effect of it can lend into a serious tornado. The good Lord invented the true colors of the rainbow in heaven. There's so many golden halos. God's lovely rain can turn into an ocean wave and rescue a fish off a shore that deserves to be saved.

Feelings

The tongue is the worst weapon you can have. You can make a cruel statement towards a person and make them feel sad. I don't have any kids. Imagine one of your family members telling you that God is gonna strike you dead, hearing those evil words really got to my head. The person told me that reminds me of the devil that enjoys wearing red. I remember going on my first date, the guy who took me out showed a whole bunch of hate. My wounds are healing, my personal reactions do turn into strange feelings. My heart always let me know when I'm in love with somebody, but every time I fall in love, the person is the opposite of a white dove. I seem to have a strange eye for the wrong guys, but one thing I will tell you, when the person is in my presence they give me so many wonderful butterflies. I can read between the lines, and I can tell when a man is full of dirty lies. Your personality may be nice, but a girl like me is very wise. Sometimes in life, love can be blind. If I dated a guy and I found out he already has somebody else in his life, when I catch him, trust me, brother, you don't have to hide. But one thing I will tell you, eventually somebody else will definitely be mine. That special someone will be my sunshine. Even if things weren't meant to work out, what is the point of crying because through the power of God. Only the strong will survive.

Rhythm

Feel the rhythm of a brand new millennium. If the man of my dreams passed away, I would surely miss him, especially if he got blasted in the face with a big silver pistol. This rhyme is dedicated to all the people who left my life, I would surely miss you. I learned how to let go, then row with the flow. I refuse to allow a man put me out there as a hoe. I have been teased about being in a self-contained class. The girl down the street considered me as being slow. Lyrically this next verse can be spiritual. Jesus Christ is my number one friend. I will never put Him before any man. The rap of my realistic thoughts travel through outer space, and I wish the evil memories of my past will fly away without a trace. The remains of a person's body can dissolve into cremation. I love the history of the Russian language. The cries in my lonely eyes always break down and raining. Some people in the world are very prejudiced, if you look back in time there is so much evidence. Life is a big lesson, there were times in my life that I almost got arrested. I never went to jail, so that was a huge blessing. This young girl fell in love with this green eyed deaf musician. The rhythm of his music was gonna take her on a mission. She wanted to be heard and she wanted him to listen. I seldom run after guys that are definitely not my type, but at the end of the day, God will show me what's wrong and what's right.

My Imagination Running Wild

I saw this older guy once before, every time I look at this older guy I fall in love with him even more. The love I have for him takes my heart on a traveling tour. I'm caught up in a situation that's strange. At this moment I do not even know his full name. Every guy I ever loved is mysterious like Monopoly, like a game. I never thought the day my choice of men would change. The look in his hazel eyes brings happiness to my cries, no matter what happens, my love will never die. Being in his presence my energy level becomes very nervous. He's a hard working man that lives in a city that's urban. I can look at him and tell he's not perfect, but I don't know if a guy like him is even worth it. I never had a long conversation with him, so I'm not the one who could judge him. The lust in his beautiful hazel eyes tells the truth, no lies. If you kindly say hello to him, he will respond to you very nice. I have been disappointed by so many guys, but I know at the end of the day, my spirit will rise. The thought of him just penetrates through my mind. I wonder will this unconditional love get buried or stay alive? Every time I walk out of his presence I always tell him goodbye, because I know the next day he will look at me and say hi. There's something about this man that's forcing me to fall in love with him, but my heart won't explain to me why.

Legend

What if a legend was born to win a beauty pageant? Imagine making history, then your story would turn out to be a mystery. Your face is in the encyclopedia and you're getting chased by the media. Your statue and picture are in the hall of fame. Each day, you're getting richer, literature made you even more famous. You came into this world born as a star, your performance took you very far. Your brilliance took you to the top, it seems like you never stop. The day you passed away and died, your fans joined hands together and cried. Your musical lyrics never lied. The world knows your not on earth physically, but you're in our minds mentally, you shall live forever spiritually. I wrote a poem about you in my journal and your memory is very eternal. The day you took your last breath, your music and voice never left.

Determination

Surly we live, we all have life, you need some kind of determination to find your desire. I'm not trying to be a liar. To set your goals for the generation. You can be anything in the world and shock the whole entire nation. Think more about your determination so you can find your desire. Find a key to unlock the knowledge and let it out of your mind so you can shine. And after you unlock it, you will never be left behind. Don't give haters what they want, keep your head up high. Your determination can inspire your hopes for the future. Say goodbye to the people's lies. Determine that one day you will wake up and your great knowledge will turn out to be wise. Show the whole world who you really are then they will realize your determination has found the right path and their pressure of trying to stop your determination shall always die.

Ghetto Love

Ghetto love can be tough or it can be penniless and rough. A lover shooting a bullet in your brain can lead you to handcuffs. Sometimes a woman just had enough. People need to look up the definition of love. A man six foot four smacking you all over the house, push comes to shove. You might pass on and fly away like a white dove. An appealing angel flying up to heaven over the rainbow. Ghetto love can have you six feet deep, resting in peace, saying your final goodbyes by a priest. Making unconditional love affection without using a condom or protection. The night of the presidential election, the man of your dreams has the ability to make a personal connection. Walking in the park after dark can give the two lovers the opportunity to make love with words. Right next to the graffiti wall colored by a spray paint artist.
Fear is beating at your heart rate because you're

extremely scared to ask a pretty girl out on a cheap date. While a cheeseburger and fries are sitting on your plate, watching a popular boy at school settle down in a romantic relationship can bring out a bunch of hate. Rapture can hurt like an innocent victim who just got raped. Endearment in the hood can do some good, like having romantic love in a spot that's abandoned. Five years later, Jim fan finally get off of the plane and get a kiss from his fiancée Janet. Going on an extended long walk is an opportunity, so two young lovers can put their heads together and talk. Ghetto love can be rough, but it can be more than enough.

Spontaneous

Goodbye, lovely yesterday, life is gonna go on each and every day. What's going on, morning? I hope today don't turn out to be boring. It's raining, it's pouring, I wonder do famous stars enjoy touring. Let's turn to the next chapter I have a lot of unwanted rapture buried deep into my heart. My brain is wounded with unfavorable marks. I've been loved by so many guys, this is my opinion, devotion never dies. The sounds that comes to my ears is tired of hearing lies. The ocean sea river will some day have the ability to rise. The cries that I have hidden will always stay inside. As long as God keeps me alive on this earth, my love will always stay alive.

Beauty is in the Eyes of the Beholder

I believe beauty is in the eyes of the beholder, let me open the truth in this folder. I started seeing discrimination in the world as I got older. The beauty is a big judgment by the naked eye. I have my days where I don't understand why. I believe society would be more kind if every female on this earth was pleasing and kind. The world seems to respect higher class people as being rich as a million dollar dime. Looks are very deceiving, people really don't understand the true meaning. A person can be very ugly, but they might have an incredible voice when it come down to singing. When you really look at a person, what do you see? Seeing an exquisite person, what do you see? Seeing an ugly person can be teasing, but through the power of God, all looks are beautiful through the eyes of Jesus.

Dominate the Challenge

A baby will not be able to be born without the sperm of men. A child should not be knowing about romantic love at the age of ten. I don't think unrighteous people understand a true meaning of a sin. A poet can write a story about their whole life with a pen. The thoughts of a human being can even escape their own fantasy about making love in an alley. Imagine being the most popular cheerleader dancing in a pep rally. Boys dream about having the most attractive girl they they can find. After you approach her, will her reactions be kind? Ever since I was a little girl, I heard that love is blind. A person can look you in the eye and the words that escape out of their mouth can be full of lies. Experiencing pain from another individual can make you very wise. Ignorance and stupidity will try to break you down like the hot humidity. Dominate the challenge on an S.A.T. test even if you have a learning disability.

Virginity

There's a reason why there's so many abortions, disease, and HIVs, because society love to give away their virginity. I think being a virgin is nourishing to the body and mind. Abstinence until marriage is better than struggling to provide a baby, a carriage. Life is all about learning to survive. Behaving the feeling of sex is better than unwrapping a condom that's latex. A virgin is preventing S.T.Ds and pregnancies because they are saving their virginity. The reason why being a virgin is nourishing is because it's better than giving money to the abortions. Everybody is not so fortunate. Sex causes hurt, distress, and it will definitely make you depressed. A broken virginity is nothing to be joking about. I believe when a woman is a virgin until marriage it all comes from courage. Catching a sexually transmitted disease is like taking away the breeze from the trees. For God's sake, we all make mistakes. My feelings would love to put the icing on the cake. When I'm around somebody I like, I might feel a little horny. But, if I decide to get pregnant by one of them, my life will be totally ruined.

Yes, Let Us Know

Our ancestors were brought to America as slaves, but you were so brave to run for president. You got good health care and the right medicine and that is a wonderful blessing. You taught the black American race a humungous lesson. No matter what color, we can stand tall and become a teacher or an architect after all. You let the whole world know we can achieve if we just believe. I just want to rule over my ambitions, instead of having a minimum wage job washing dishes. Yes, we can pursue a dream, we can definitely be as successful as a king.

You let us know we can be anything we want, we just have to hunt for the knowledge. We can take a long journey to college. You have a big influence on people in general. It was a miracle when you got elected. On that amazing day, I felt like going in my closet and dancing around in one of my expensive jackies. No matter what people say, we can break our fear and become the first black mear. We can also share our game of knowledge. I will always respect you because you didn't even hesitate to have courage and stay strong. You did what you had to to stand tall. The day you ran for president I knew you had a successful plan, I will have respect for you because you are a strong black. Even the unemployed men can stand tall, too.

Disappointment

The world is full of disappointment, especially when a rich suburban girl's family found out she fell in love with a man who was collecting unemployment. A young girl with a broken heart should wash away her tears and keep on moving. Famous football players get faced off with a lot of disappointment, especially when the game turns out to be ruined. A pretty woman can get disappointed by a handsome bachelor when he is only concerned about the moment of joy and laughter. I lived through a car accident, I was very disappointed when the lenses fell out of my glasses. Life is full of action. Love can turn a mistress into a fatal attraction. She may teach her lover a lesson by making his life unpleasant. Her heart is filled up with so much pain. It will be very scary if she shot him and the bullet went directly to his brain. Now he's six feet under, resting in his grave. The only thing she can do is ask for forgiveness in Jesus' name. Disappointment is going to occur in her life. The day she got arrested, I pray that the next step won't be going to the penitentiary, and getting molested. The good Lord will never disappoint you, His eternal love will always be everlasting.

The Love of Languages

God loves languages more than the Jamaican fishes in the deep blue sea. God gave me a clue to see the future of speaking foreign languages. It was a boring day, God saved me a morning of having a love for languages. God loves languages more than the air force mountains are high. I believe an interpreter spirit is high, like a beautiful butterfly in the sky. Every new language is gonna be a new lesson. But the life I'm living is just a beautiful blessing. God loves languages more the peaceful place of Rome. I know God loves languages more than the marines of Jordan.

Friendship

The most beautiful thing about living life is having a close relationship that can follow into friendship. People that walk on land will talk to you on the phone, to start a real friendship with you. As time goes by, you will find the actual truth about this human being. Now the friendship you had with this person has fallen apart. Sadness has passed into a cry tears. Back stabbing friends have always been this way for years. Deep down inside you thought you had a true friend with the kind of heart that cares. Jesus Christ wants to come into your life to share a real friendship with you that shall treasure deep into your heart and soul forever. Never give up on your faith, Jesus will always be with you, even until the end of the universe. My dear best friend, thank You for dying on the cross for my sin now. I'm safe from the fire breathing dragon. I don't need a friend, I got God and His Messiah as a friend.

Poem

Courage can be inevitable. A white dove is incredible. In my desire I wish I can borrow a few seconds from tomorrow. Our last day of life is the beginning of sorrow. The voice of thunder can create a whole world full of lightning. Poetry is a form of writing. My love is conscientiousness, the fine lyrics of a poem are splendid, waking up in the morning is a new beginning. A fighter earning a championship is doing nothing but winning. The wings of a butterfly will never tell no lies. The cries of a river sea ocean will some day rise. All my life I've been faced with so many goodbyes.

Missing Affection

We had a special connection, the love was more than unconditional affection. All of my life I had been faced off with rejection. My heart is split in half. I hope my love doesn't go down the wrong path. What is the point of sharing your troubles with a friend? They might turn their back on you and laugh. I hope you are listening, my affection is missing, the sun is raising after dawn. Would the love of your life walk out the door? Then all of a sudden, the feelings they had for you are gone. Hurting an individual is wrong, especially if you and this person had a special bond.

Dirty Church Member

Instead of coming to church and praising the Lord, he's attempting to become an undercover church whore. I guess he's happily married, but it seems like he wants more. As soon as church was over, I immediately ran out the door. He tries to talk over my life. Then all of a sudden, I get unexpected phone calls from his wife. The good Lord knows that I want peace. One time he called my house, and told my father that he was looking for his niece. I've been writing this book for almost five years. When I read the poem in front of church, it sounded very weird. This is my opinion, I don't think it was a poem that people wanted to hear. Every time I write a poem, the only thing I can write about is the truth. His wife told me I should write my poetry for the young youth. One time he followed me to the water fountain, then when I looked up, he was standing right there. When this situation happened, his wife was sitting in the church. This man definitely did not care. Some things in life there is a limit. I remember sitting in the church, I was trying to listen to the pastor. He snuck in and took my picture without my permission. I don't believe this man is a real Christian. I need you to listen. I bet you there is something in his life that is definitely missing. One Sunday my dad and I decided to leave church early. Then I got up and he looked at me and said, "You leaving? What about the Christmas play?" When something is going on in my life, this man always has something to say. Older men bother me every day. This man just doesn't know that I have a bad temper. I just had to get this situation off my mind and write a poem about this dirty church member.

30 Days

I had only been here for thirty days when I found the girl in the next apartment building was gay. I found out a new, exciting thing every day. My best friend got pregnant and aborted her baby away. The girl next door was pregnant, so she say, comes to find out she was five months all day. A perm face woman wanted me to give my sex away. I decided to stay a virgin, I'll stay. These stupid ass boys don't know what to say to a real woman. If you were a hoe, they will come out to play. The maintenance man was a drunk all day long, and the landlord used his crack cocaine to do his wrong. Listen to my summer vacation in my song. I thought it was going to be fun, but it turned out to be wrong. Naggas was saying I was the softest one in the room, they don't even know me from the man on the moon. They're mad because I don't want to get freak too soon. All I want to do is stay in school and let them dance to the beat of my groove. If you prove yourself to these people, you will definitely lose. That's why I've written all this bad news.

The Clear Blue Sky

Every time I look up at the clear blue sky, I know there's a living God that lives somewhere over the clouds on earth, it's so loud. A woman can be proud to give birth to an innocent child. The nurse will wrap the baby up in a small towel, then the baby will give the nurse a little smile. An airplane can be miles away from land, far away from man. When I look up at the clear blue sky, I know souls never die. Sunset may fall into night and tomorrow there will be light.

Emotions

When a man and a woman is making romantic love, it can run into emotions, from the touch to the feel of heart warming love. I am an emotional young woman, some heart warming love can make you feel like a beautiful white dove, that our Lord and Savior Jesus Christ created from above. Tear drops are crying from the hurt of a child that lost her virginity to a man that forgot about her and her beautiful eternal love. Heart breaking love can fill your soul with hate. It can make you forget about your dream and goals like a high above rain drop, washing away the wish from a heart warming adventure shooting star.

Life Shell

God plants a child in the mother's women for a reason. Each season a child is being born to see the moonlight, soon they will be living in the afternoon. When a baby is finally born, they will no longer be living in their little room. Living in life shell can be like writing a fairy tail. Dreaming to hear the sound of the wedding bells reminds me of a snail trying to come out of his seashell. When a person passes away, the spirit of the soul transform out of their little bowl and fly over into the crossroad. There can be all kinds of rumors about a dead person's body, the person that lived in that body just recently came back from a house party. Our body is the temple of God, to other people that sounds kind of odd. Adam and Eve ate the apple from the tree. If everybody in this world lived by God's commandments, their life will never feel abandoned. Worldly people that disobey God's commandments remind me of a plane that never landed.

Rhyme

Poetry can be very emotionable, you can write a story about a girl being antisociable. I am in pain, I have a lot of knowledge in my brain. My life is very miserable, ever since I could remember, I always been foolish and sensible. Young boys are the masters of getting physical. My determination is my hero. Poetry can create a rhyme about remembering the time. When a famous star got signed, from the beginning the manager just knew you would shine. Heal the spirit of the graffiti, rap lyric, the innocent children playing hopscotch can hear it. Butterscotch cannot make an unsightly girl pretty and hot. Poetry is the rhyme of dime lemon lime. The feeling of poetry can be extraordinary and kind. A boy can write you a poem and it can say be my Valentine. Who created the rhymes of lyrics? People would try to turn endearment into a science experiment. People try to turn love into action, maybe they just want to see your reaction.

Infatuation

I did not expect to fall back into an infatuation, the boy that I'm infatuated with has a twin bother named Mason. This boy is cuter than a special occasion. It's so amazing how you can discover that you have a crush, and recover from your mistakes. For God's sake, never tell nobody which boy you're infatuated with. Every day he walks past my Spanish class, my reactions turn into beautiful butterflies, and that is no lie. Just being in his presence, my feelings turn so emotionable and shy. He is such a kindhearted person. Sometimes I fantasize being with him, but I know it's just a young girl's infatuation. I know going out with him will not be a success, unless I express myself to him in a way that I don't want to do.

Slow of Speech

Ever since I was three, I began to stutter. I was too young to understand what was wrong with my speech, so there were no other great scientist in the world that can find a cure for my stammering. It feels like an enormous nail is hammering my voice, so I cannot have the knowledge or the ability to make some noise. Stuttering doesn't make you slow or dumb. You may stumble on some words when you're feeling extremely depressed. Express yourself and speak, don't allow others to make you sad or weak. I know stuttering seemed bad, but look at it like this, we can stand on our own two feet and walk. But most of the time, it can be very difficult for us to talk. I understand how it feels when words are being blocked. No matter what people say, just push your words out and talk.

Thug Passion

After reading the Webster's Dictionary, I understand why music sounds like black history, society, and the world thought you were a mystery. You were an American thug legend, your raps made life pleasant. You told the truth about life, reality, and its magical youth. Your deep musical stories will never be boring. You had the potential to write a book about a young boy in the penitentiary who cannot read a book up to sixth grade elementary. When you rap about the next century being risky, your rhymes gave your lyrics so much inspiration, so the melody of your creative beats became busy. You wore a bulletproof vest, because you didn't want your time on earth to get blast in a hearse. People thought you were cursed, but it could have been worst. You had the mind to explain why being a black man might make you inferior, but if you believe it, can make you superior. I never knew rap music could talk about a drug dealer getting capped. Your music went all over the world map, because it's so deep. Your musical lyrics made the definition of violence weep. You were born to be a philosopher, but the world wanted to turn you into a monster. Little did they know you had the mind of an author. The law made you feel it's deep. Your musical lyrics made the definition of violence weep. You were born to be a philosopher, but the world want to you into a monster, little did they know you had the mind of a author. The law made you feel like a foster child, because you are a black man. Your memory will not be remembered as a cemetery. Your raps will live forever spiritually. I bet your tongue could rap about a dancer marrying a veterinarian. Every time I look above, I know fear is stronger than love. You were a thug angel that flew away like a white dove. When it came to just being you, you were the best. Rest in peace.

Remember the Night Forever

Prom night, remember the night forever. A night to be desirable and requireable to enter. There will be a winner as a king and queen, eventually you will come out of those jeans to put on your fashionable bow and tie. The girls will walk in the prom with their impressible hair style, everybody will say wow! Some of the other girls in the crowd will have on glittery dresses that will make them look fabulous and impressive. The silver ball in the middle of the dance floor will be glowing. People will be acting a fool and showing off. The popular girls will be posing for the year book, with their pretty looks. Couples will be hugging to the slow song, for that particular moment, the two of them will have a special bond. They may feel like there's nothing wrong with having premarital sex after the prom. There will be all kinds of laughter, bastard children will be getting conceived. Believe me, somebody will get nominated as king and queen. People will be committing abominations against God, on prom night, that sounds kind of odd. At the end of the prom, a lot of broads will get hot in the back seat of the car, in the middle of the parking lot. Remember the night forever. Some people will go home and act like they just came back from the exquisite city of Rome. Remember the night forever, a night to be handsome and jazzy, the night shall be everlasting.

Lust

The world around me thinks I'm a little kid. I know one thing, if you break God's commandments, you are committing a sin. At the age I am right now, I have a sexual desires for older men. A romantic relationship will never be perfect, like Barbie and Ken. I'm 21 years old and I'm still a virgin. I don't know when I'm ever gonna have sex. I couldn't even tell you when. I started my period at the age of ten and I truly believe that I have strong feelings for the wrong men. My way of thinking is the only way I can find trust. What is the meaning of pure lust? My sexual desires move on to a different route. A newlywed couple have all night to have sex all over their house. If a man ever steps on my heart, I will leave him and fly down south. Pure lust will make you wanna have an affair, but when you leave your spouse for your lover, your lover will attempt to make you care. The hurt in my eyes cried more than one tear. I know I'm a virgin, but I fall in love with my sexual desires every year. Love is not young or old, older men turn me on. This pretty handsome man told me that my hair looks lovely. I don't care what anybody says, I am no where ugly. I have not met the right man that I can actually trust, but at the end of the day, I am a human being that go through a period of lust.

Backbone

Having a backbone begins with loving the Lord, but it's in your determination that will give you much more. People do grow up poor. Without accepting Christ in your heart, you will surely fall to the floor. The reason why a lot of teenage girls end up pregnant is because they don't have no backbone to teach them right from wrong. Bad habits will have you hopping for some carrots like rabbits. Children make wrong choices because they don't hear the proper words coming out of their families' voices. The sound of moaning, groaning, and making a whole bunch of noises can lead into deadly disease that's poison. Trying to achieve a career without having faith in God, one day you may come up, then all of a sudden, your dream fell over and died. A lot of kids don't make it to their high school graduation. The hard headed ones are out there in the streets or resting in their grave. Believing in strength will make you very brave. Living life without a backbone might make you feel all alone. A teenage girl may express herself by wearing body piercings and talking to boys on the phone. The poor girl doesn't have no backbone to teach her right from wrong. There is so much destruction going on at home. When she graduated from high school, she joined the U.S. military, then moved to the country Rome. Her whole life story is like writing a chapter in a poem.

Trauma

I took a bus ride to visit another town, because I was curious and I wanted to look around. Let me explain to you what happened to me right now. I was having a nice day, coming from Chick-Fil-A. I walked across the street, not expecting any drama. When I seen this luxury car coming towards me, I knew this situation was going to be trauma. I cracked the windshield, and thank God, I didn't get killed. In a situation like this, the only thing I can do is keep it real. I got thrown up in the air and landed on my face. I broke my glasses and the lenses landed all over the place. My teeth got chipped, and I had a swollen bloody lip. My body was aching because the car took me on a trip.

The driver got out of the car and started yelling at me. His reaction to the whole situation was taking him too far. The driver called the rescue squad out of fair. I knew I was going to the hospital, but I didn't know where. I overheard the cops telling the paramedic that the man was driving at forty-five. Through the power of God, I'm still alive. The moment I got hit by the car, I just knew I wasn't going to die. When the paramedic brought me inside the hospital, I felt like a helpless baby crying for a bottle. If the doctors would have taken me to surgery, I wouldn't have even been worried.

But everything turned out to be okay, the nurse put me inside of a machine they can give me an x-ray. I just want you to understand what I'm trying to say, this turned out to be a bad day. I got released from the hospital then the next day. I made an appointment to see the dentist. I need you to listen, my teeth got chipped very bad. Every time I looked at myself in the mirror, I felt very sad. The following week, when the dentist worked on my teeth, I felt very proud, because I can finally take a picture of myself and smile. I'm the type of girl that enjoys smiling and laughing, but I never thought that day I would live through a car accident.

Urban

Growing up in a town that's urban, hardly any foreigners are German. Low lifed parents be out there in the streets, lusting. Why their children be going to school fussing? Young drug dealers be out there in the streets selling crack cocaine, without understanding that knowledge is very important to have in your brain. There's kids in the hood that dream of fortune and fame, the hard headed ones give up their aspirations and stay the same. Take a look back at their parents, they are to blame. Living life in the hood is not like playing a monopoly game. What if a pregnant girl walks into her high school class room? Her teacher might look down on her with shame without understanding her cries and pain. What if she worked on being an actor in Hollywood, then one year later, her movie made it to the big screen and show, she has a famous name. It doesn't matter if you came from the slums of the ghetto, you can still make it to the Winter Olympics and win a gold medal.

Cry

There may be a time where you feel like your heart is beating out of your chest because evil words from another person's mouth created a sword, stabbing deep into your flesh. Rapture is all about communication and trust. Telling the love of your life goodbye can hurt the human eye. Have you ever felt like you wanted to die? Excitement can lead into a bundle of cries, but never give up the effort to tr. If God gave me wings, I will open them and fly. Love can happen in many different forms. Tears from an ocean sea river can wash away a storm. Unexpected things happen on a college dorm. Every time I cry, my eyes feel very warm. If a man left me for another woman, my eyes will be crushed and torn, especially if I knew she was pregnant with his baby that will someday be born.

Sincere

Being sincere is being truly honest, that you have a successful career. The sound of singing birds' music can penetrate through a person's ear. Where is the love? The race of humanity seems to care. Going through an emotional break up can form into a tear. One minute people are this way, then the next minute people are very dishonest about being in love with a ridiculous man. What is the point of being in a committed relationship, then all of a sudden you decide to go out there and cheat? A situation like this can increase the speed of the heartbeat. When it's time for people to be sincere about what they have to say, they act like their tongue is too quiet to speak. The definition of sincere is deep. It hurts really bad when a man decides not to tell the truth to his lady, because he wants to run around like a dog and not be faithful. The word sincere reminds me of the true colors of the rainbow. There are people in this world that live their whole life being a liar. When the moment comes for them to tell the truth, will they be required? Some people in this world today, retire from the truth.

Living life as an entity, and going through magical youth, reminds me of a child losing their first tooth. A person can take a lie detector test and they can never hide from the truth, because this little machine has a whole lot of proof.

Eternal Love Forever

Eternal love forever, every time I look above, you never shove me away. What I'm trying to say, you will always be the number one Man. You carry the whole world in Your hands. Sometimes in life, I fear that I'm never gonna become successful, but that just crazy lies coming from the devil. Lord, I know You will always have my back the way this way world is today, temptation will try to attack. Every time my prayers knock on heaven's door, You send me wonderful blessings back. Having faith in God will guide you to the land of hope. Never allow trials and tribulations, to wash your dreams out with soap. I prayer that You lift my confidence up. God, I try to stay away from people who are messed up and corrupt. Men who are creating their own laws for the world trying to make life rough. The devil wants more, he doesn't want enough. Believing in the power of courage will make your heart tough.

I can write a novel about my childhood memories. One day, the Lord our King will be back for all our family.

The Thirteen-Year-Old

There lived this thirteen-year-old girl with a severe learning disability, her vocabulary level sounds like a child. That's beginning, in the early years of third grade elementary. If you try to make some effort into putting some knowledge into her head, it might take you into the next century. She's very stubborn and silly. This little thirteen-year-old girl is six months pregnant by her boyfriend Billy. Her father is nowhere in her life, he left her when she was just a toddler, then he went on to the U.S. military. He got married and started a new life in Philly. The thirteen-year-old girl threw away all of her goals, the only thing she cares about is chasing her boyfriend Billy. He's headed down the wrong road. The thirteen-year-old girl could have prevented this situation by just saying no.

Emotions

When a man and a woman are making romantic love, it can run into emotions from the touch, to the feel of heart warming love. It can make you feel like a beautiful white dove that our Lord and Savior Jesus Christ created from above. Tear drops are crying from a child who lost her virginity to a man, that forgot about her and her beautiful eternal love. Heart breaking love can fill your soul with hate. It can make you forget about your dreams and goals, like a high above rain drop, wash away the wish from a heart warming adventure shooting star.

Sticks and Stones

Sticks and stones may break my bones, but bringing who you are will always work. I walk into my high school hallway and I am standing alone. My thoughts would tell me I hope the school day don't turn out to be wrong. It's a shame how young human being show the educated world that I don't care about you and your stupid rules. Test scores are poor. Low grade averages are sure that you will definitely drop out of high school stupid. People that are on the honor roll hall of fame seem to be this ugly scientist, looking lame to society. I try to be with the team popularity. I just say forget it and buy more knowledge will always remain in the back of my mind. Sticks and stones may break my bones, but being who you are will always work.

Rap is Poetry

A famous rapper knows how to rap about poetry. You're constantly timing and rhyming the words taste very delicious. After you get done writing, I bet you feel magnificent. All the work and effort you put into that poem, I bet you feel like you should have won some kind of certificate. Poetry can talk about how a little girl saw a disinterested murder. The situation hurt her so much, the boy was brutally, cruelly beaten. The funeral was extremely sad. Poetry can rap about a poor little girl being mad. It's a shame how a rapper can rap about a person getting capped. Dang, you act like the rhyme was trapped from pregnancy and you had to call the emergency. You know surgery rhymes with poetry and rhymes with crime. Wow, poetry has a whole new kind of rap.

War

Forever the Marines will stay alive to show North Korean beautiful pride. Little Clear'ra cried just to be the bride of a handsome, good looking majesty. For all the Marines, goodbyes must fight to stay alive. Little Bre-ann tried to hide from the nuclear weapon that's gonna rise. Forever and ever, the people that live in terror will find the heart and courage to survive.

Double Lesson

Becoming a parent is a double lesson, especially if you're going through a stage of adolescent devotion that will never fad away. A fatal attraction can cause a whole bunch of action, they can amuse another person's reaction. A variable person can have so many plants, but they might have a hard time loving again. Once the future comes, a nineteen-year-old girl will be romantically in love with a real man. This young girl and this guy dated, but the love they have for each other will always be incarcerated.

True Life Poetry

A writer is nothing but a fighter, especially when it's time for the lyrics to jump higher. True life poetry is real, it's not a liar. My entire life has told a story of poetry, sometimes poetry can be emotionable. When the revelation of Christ comes back, there will be no discrimination to judge all humanity. It will not be like eating a piece of candy. The word of God is a part of society. A lot of children come to school every day, being hilarious and their teacher doesn't understand what's going on in their life, so their thoughts become very curious. I will be so embarrassed, if I allow my dearest dream to turn into steam. Sometimes true life poetry has to turn mean, especially when you want the lyrics to win the fight in the boxing ring.

Sense of Humor

Having a sense of humor means to be comical. A comedian's jokes can be funny and powerful. The audience may think the show is delightful, sitting in the front row seat I would be frontful. The characteristic of realistic laughter can show spontaneous emotions, like a witch stirring some potion. A furious frown turned upside down can also be ready. Let the truth hit the ground, so they can win the peace and honor crown. I wonder when does a comedian stop telling wisecracks? Never. Standing on stage, the comedian can make the audience laugh because they like the joke about the dog cage. A moment of being phenomenal, the joke can be incredible, maybe it will be reasonable. Falling to your knees in the dirt, because your stomach hurt from a crazy joke. A true comedian was born to write some funny notes. There's a song called Rock the Boat, the comedian might say Rock the Quote.

Until Death Do Us Part

The pain of sorrow is killing my heart. I'm just a young girl, going out into the world, but I don't know where to start. We all will experience the pain of sorry. I wonder, will I live to see tomorrow? I never introduce myself to a boy named Carol. Death is when the soul of the body left. Out temporary home, until we fly into Heaven's Rome. You will never feel solitary or all alone. On earth, there's millions of doggy bones. Imagine being in a place of peace and you don't even have to feel solitary or all alone.

Imagine being in a place of peace and you don't even have to pay the cost of a cell phone. Sleeping in your casket is like laying some eggs in an Easter basket. Resting without existence, what is the feeling of living? The feeling of crying and experiencing hurt, imagine watching your loved one's casket get buried in the dirt.

Unconditional love comes from above. The Lord created white doves to fly over the earth with love. The lovely rain is nature's rain showers. I wonder how does it feel to stand over heaven's towers.

My First Option

When I was fourteen years old, I was not worried about having a man. I was worried about having a plan for the future. I want to be able to pay for my kids' college tuition, so they can be successful as a pediatrician. Whatever decision, they will always have a mama that will listen. I'm perfect, I'm not a Christian, but I want to go from rags to riches. It's a shame, waking up every day and there's no food in your kitchen. Sometimes I wish I was put up for adoption, maybe I would have a better option. I watch how these young girls struggle, they don't even have a decent car seat with a buckle. It's not in my philosophy to look up the feeling of sex in the glossary. Every day, I wake up in pain like a bruised knee. But I seem to go the right direction. Me and my childhood memories have a special connection. I wanted it to be urgent, it was meant for me to be a virgin, because when I was fifteen years old, I met this boy who was so bold to call a female a hoe. I tried everything in my power to go over the Cowers' house, so I could get close to him. But, most of the time I did not have a ride, so the feeling of being with him died.

Valedictorian

I told the future of the valedictorians. It can be very incredible and glorious to see you seniors hold their victory for their future. Negativity will never stop the valedictorians from caring about their life of success. Some valedictorians have this kind of dream of being the wife of a superstar that lives in Hollywood, the beautiful city of dreams. Good grades will get you far away from living in the ghetto. Come walk through the valley of knowledge so you can take a long journey to college. You can be successful as a young intelligent attorney. Tell yourself, let there be change and rearrange your victory, fly away like an eagle, so you can soar as a valedictorian.

One Flesh

A married couple is supposed to come together as one flesh. A relationship is all about communication and trust. Sexual immorality is a deep feeling of lust. A woman's sad cries can fall into a pile of dust. Affection can make two people kiss and hold hands. People always say a man is gonna be a man. Wicked attraction can control a person's sexual desire to sin. Prostitutes don't care about making unconditional love to a married man. Evil temptation will always try to win. God made women and men so they can come together as one flesh. If you try to explain that to a young person, they might think you're nuts. Cheating on your spouse can cause a whole bunch of problems in your house. If I were committed to someone, I will still have my doubts. I don't know if he will make unconditional love to a woman with an inappropriate blouse. A man has one time to cheat on me. I will drop him like a piece of candy and run free. It seems like my poetic thoughts is suddenly growing like a flower on a tree.

Hoping, Dreaming, and Wishing

Hoping, dreaming, and wishing will take you on a mission. Learning how to cope with a situation, and hoping for a better life, will take you on a journey. Dreaming to become successful as an attorney will take your brain far away on a train. Wishing to have the ultimate amount of money is like fighting with a bunch of hungry bees to catch the honey. A lot of followers that follow behind the leader may have a passion for fashion. Sometimes in life, you have to beat down an ignorant team to pursue your dreams. God is an inspiration to people's heart, soul, mind, and body. Some people don't know how to find the right direction to hope. I feel like I'm in an election, wishing to get voted as president. So I can sign the bill to get the right medicine. Except I'm hoping, dreaming, and wishing to get a blessing that will make dreams come true. Your intelligence has to be the boss of dreams, like a captain being in charge of a basketball team.

Aqua Falls

Oh, God's green earth, He created the magic wall, so a bird or dragonfly can fly through the beautiful Niagara Falls. Wind breezes are cold, the aqua falls have frozen deep ocean waves. Will never save a human being's life from drowning beyond the magic wave. Waterfalls keep the earth from being dry. Rivers, lakes, and oceans will fill with rain that falls out of the sky. Half-human fish will always have a wish to talk upon the shore line and adore the steps they left behind. Aqua falls shall be everlasting for all.

Mercy

I forgive and I will forget. I'm gonna have to admit that sometimes it's hard to forgive and forget. The good Lord would be happy if you give mercy on others more than a little bit. Imagine if your enemy killed one of your closest siblings? Would you do something to that person to make them pay? Listen to my rhyme, because God does say vengeance is Mine. Forgive your enemy, never give up trying. Just light a candle then pray over your loved one's soul. The person who killed your loved one was cruel and bold. Don't show no hate, love your enemy, and forgive them. Trust me, I know it's hard. Pretend the good Lord just sent you a post card and wrote, "My dear child, forgive your enemy. I really care that you do." Teaching another person how to hate is wrong. Keep on praying then, you will definitely grow strong.

From the Inside and Out

As I got older, I tried to push away off of my pain over my shoulder. I learned how to love myself from the inside and out. Sometimes I have doubts about the way I look, but I shook those demands away and said, "Hey, you're beautiful no matter what people say." I never learned how to play marbles, my skin complexion is light skin caramel. My beautiful eyes are dark brown. I glow as a queen wearing a crown. If you listen to my voice, it sounds like I'm trying to make some noise. My lips are a nice size, they also stay dry in the winter time. It's all up to me to keep them moist with Vaseline. I spray my braided hair with Oil Sheen. My hands are the boss of my hair, every time I put water on my hair it becomes very thick and curly. Every single day I wake up very early. I used to be a sophomore in high school. I remember styling my hair in a nice hair bun. Soon as I cruise down the hallway, the sight of everybody's eyes pays attention to my hair because it's always done. The moment I decide to pull my hair back in a ponytail, all of you will see coin silk waves, but most of the times I wear my hair in braids. My great-grandmother was a full blooded Indian. I'm very petite with a nice shape. Sometimes, I wish I can hide my body with a cape. As a woman, I'm never going to allow a man take advantage of me, for God's sake. I believe everybody should keep their mind focused on school, but deep down inside I know there's no way I can change the world. I have great plans for my future, so the knowledge in my mind can become smarter and huger.

Don't

Don't judge a book by its cover, it can be about two lovers. A young girl might walk down the street wearing a pair of Daisy Dukes, but that doesn't mean she's sexually active with a man. Next time you see her, don't judge because she's wearing a pair of tight jeans and sneakers. People will try to make you feel bad and weakers. You don't have to take their judgment into consideration. People will judge the way you look at a special occasion. Some people will judge a foreigner because they may not understand the English language. It's amazing how you can go to school to be a judge, a fudgsicle until they open their mouth and taste it. Don't waste your time listening to a person that's gonna throw stones at you because you're in love with a pro basketball player that's six feet tall. All bad people do is beat each other down in a fight, they will definitely judge who won and who lost the fight. Only God can judge mankind. People don't realize, let God judge what he created. Most people will judge a stripper that's shaking and twisting her body on a pole. She's living in a dog-eat-dog world, being called a sinner. Nobody is a winner when they judge. Allow God to do His work, because He's the one who created the world.

www.ingramcontent.com/pod-product-compliance
Lightning Source LLC
Chambersburg PA
CBHW060405050426
42449CB00009B/1909